# POOLS

DESIGN AND FORM
WITH WATER

*Thanks to Claudia Matheja for her dedication from the start, to Gärtner von Eden and other designers and installers for their excellent projects, to Ignacio Pujol of Ara Grup for his advice on natural pools, and to the team at The Images Publishing Group.*

# POOLS

## DESIGN AND FORM
## WITH WATER

**Miquel Tres**
In collaboration with Claudia Matheja

images
Publishing

Edited by Sabita Naheswaran

Published in Australia in 2014 by
The Images Publishing Group Pty Ltd
ABN 89 059 734 431
6 Bastow Place, Mulgrave, Victoria 3170, Australia
Tel: +61 3 9561 5544  Fax: +61 3 9561 4860
books@imagespublishing.com
www.imagespublishing.com

National Library of Australia Cataloguing-in-Publication entry:

Author:          Tres, Miquel
Title:           Pools: design and form with water / Miquel Tres.
ISBN:            9781864705867 (hardback)
Subjects:        Swimming pools – Design and construction.
                 Swimming pools – Pictorial works.
Dewey Number:    728.962

Coordinating editor: Sabita Naheswaran

Designed by Ryan Marshall, The Graphic Image Studio Pty Ltd, Mulgrave, Australia
www.tgis.com.au

Pre-publishing services by United Graphic Pte Ltd, Singapore

Printed by Everbest Printing Co. Ltd., in Hong Kong/China on 150gsm Quatro Silk

# Contents

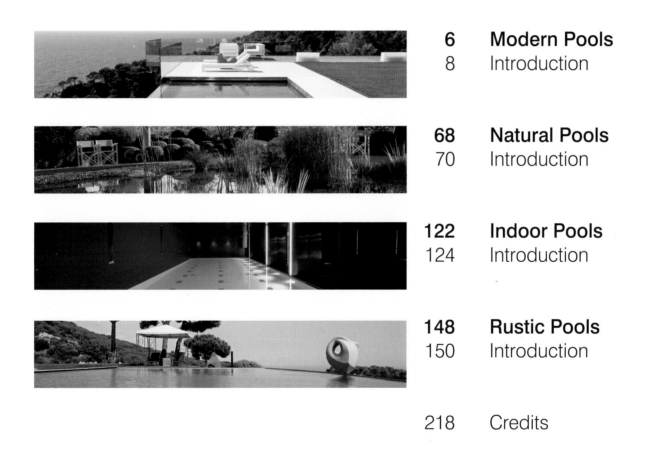

POOLS

Modern pools can be characterized by their minimalist designs, the use of straight lines, and angular features. These pools are generally

rectangular, and are sometimes constructed as swim canals more suitable for exercise than leisure. They could be located anywhere: in manicured estates, or terraces overlooking the sea, or in everyday family gardens. Often these types of pools have infinity-edges, which cascade into a lower depository. Infinity-edge pools are often directed toward stunning views so that the water surface blends with the horizon to create a spectacular visual effect.

Modern pools – of any size – offer the ultimate in technological innovations, especially regarding purification, cleansing, and security. They can feature counter-current jets, which enable their

owners to practice resistance swimming, or automatic floor cleaning systems that remove the necessity to use unsightly pool robots, which incorporate hoses that float in the water. Solar heating systems help maintain the water temperature to extend the swimming season.

To avoid heat loss and prevent leaves and dirt from polluting the pool when it is not in use, a wide range of covers are available, from simple floating blankets that extend manually, to sophisticated, remote-control operated systems hidden in pool sides.

MODERN

Modern pools are, of course, surrounded by modern accessories, including deckchairs with matching tables, stylized lights, motorized umbrellas (some of which have remote controls), stainless steel outdoor showers, or wall-mounted speakers. Outdoor furniture is usually made of aluminium, stainless steel, exotic wood, or vegetable fibres; if the pool is close to the sea, these furnishings are often reinforced, and need to be able to withstand salty, corrosive marine winds. Textiles (cushions, shade-cloths, outdoor carpets, hammocks, etc.) are constructed using nautical water-resistant fabrics.

A material that is widely accepted and has a great visual impact is micro-cement. It can be painted, and is durable enough to build surfaces and walls.

Glass is another material that is used consistently, either within pool walls to create water windows, or in adjacent areas to emphasize a sleek, contemporary overall aesthetic. Styles of paving range from big stone slabs, to ceramic tiles, while wooden decking is also popular.

The basins of modern pools can be clad in a range of colors; glass mosaic tiles have an endless variety of shades. Popular colors tend to be white, red, orange, blue, turquoise, and black. Stainless steel basins are also sought after.

Illumination plays an important role. Underwater LED spotlights are common in modern pools, as are exterior border beacons. LED spotlights come in a range of colors, and can change the overall aesthetic of a pool instantly.

POOLS

This modern, elegant pool (10.4m x 3m) was designed to mirror the line of the house and separate the long terrace into three spaces. Halogen lights were installed in waterproof wall niches, and illuminate both the pool and the terrace. The infinity-edge seems to bend toward the sea, and opens to vast views of the landscape and distant coastline. The artificial granite slabs and white mosaic tiles that form the border of this pool are complemented by dark ipe-wood decking.

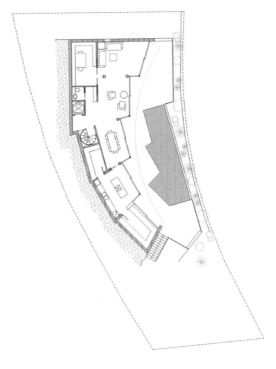

This L-shaped pool dominates the lateral facade of the house, and accompanies a small paved terrace.

The communication between the house and the pool (3.5m x 10m) is emphasized by the strictly lineal design.

The pool overflows (at its longest side) into a canal of white pebbles that contrast perfectly with the color and texture of the ipe-wood decking. It features pale turquoise mosaic tiles, a counter current system, underwater lighting, and is cleaned using salt chlorination.

This 25m² stainless steel pool has a striking aesthetic that punctuates the spectacular country setting. It features an overflowing canal, vibrant blue underwater illumination (LED), and integrates geothermal heating. The L-shaped house protects the terrace, while grasses and bamboo add color and structure, and provide visual protection. Floor-to-ceiling windows open to the pool and ipe-wood sundeck from all inside spaces.

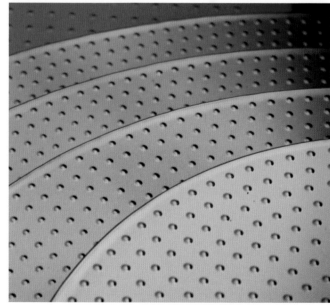

This oval-shaped pool – with an integrated jacuzzi – perched high on a coastline with spectacular views to the Mediterranean sea, belongs to a mansion in Costa Brava, and is situated on a terrace of travertine slabs. The shotcrete basin is clad in white glass mosaic tiles; all pool accessories are also white to create a sense of visual consistency.

The pool is cleaned using a salt electrolosis chemical treatment, and features 300W underwater spotlights. The jacuzzi's climate is controlled using an electric exchanger.

The design of this two-level swimming pool (12.8m x 4m and 4.5m x 4m) integrates a 3m waterfall, which pours over a slate wall to create a "water curtain". The infinity-edge removes the necessity for unsightly grids and borders, while a prefabricated concrete canal runs along the shotcrete basin so as not to disturb the aesthetic balance. The ipe-wood stairs and sundeck, the terrace, and the shaded "chill-out" area add texture and create a sense of symmetry.

Underwater illumination is provided via three LED projectors, with three basic colors: red, blue, and green; by combining these, a total of 12 colors can be created. The ivory-colored glass mosaic tiles were chosen in order to emphasize these different color illuminations.

The water is treated chemically using salt electrolysis, a process that uses dissolved salt to store chlorine which, using electrolysis, then produces sanitizing agents. The pool also utilizes an automatic floor cleaning system. Plants of varying heights were distributed in order to provide visual protection, and create an exotic, resort-like feel.

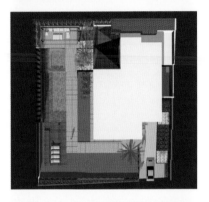

The slope on which this house was built serves to create various garden terraces and emphasizes stunning panoramic views of the northern coast of Barcelona. The pool is accessed via railway sleepers that lead down to the lower terrace.

The 8m x 4m infinity-edge pool features metallic grey mosaic tiles that shimmer when the water is in motion. A striking stainless steel ladder contrasts the ipe decking.

This 40-year-old mansion close to Tossa de Mar sits above a rocky coast with unbelievable views over Costa Brava, and has direct access to a small beach. The spectacular scenery facilitated the creation of flexible indoor-outdoor spaces: the new outdoor dining room can also be used as a terrace and, if needed, can be closed to the elements using large, sliding, floor-to-ceiling glass doors. A water basin – with a small water cascade – sits to one side of the dining room, and stone stools were utilized so the owners and guests can sit in the water.

The old triangular swimming pool was removed and substituted with a rectangular infinity pool which seems to pour into the sea. It measures 12m x 4m, features underwater LED illumination and marine blue tiles, and is cleaned using a skimmer and salt electrolysis. A whirlpool jacuzzi at the entrance to the pool is protected by a pull-out sun roof with built-in showers and loudspeakers.

This recently renovated house in Sant Cugat (close to Barcelona) has a 300m² garden. Its kidney-shaped pool was inspired by the Lanzarote Island pools of architect and artist Cesar Manrique. Constructed of shotcrete, it was finished in white waterproof and non-slip powder corundum (grade three), which requires no maintenance.

The pool is heated using solar energy, and disinfected using ultraviolet light and liquid oxygen. It utilizes a traditional skimmer and nozzle system, and has two remote-control operated LED projectors which change colour. A bench was integrated into the stairs.

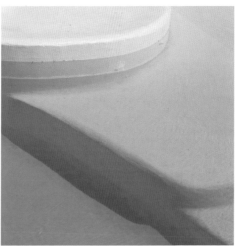

This family home was built on a small plot, however the owners' desired a large pool with a maximum water surface. The result was an 8m x 3m rectangular pool – constructed of shotcrete – visually integrated with the living area via large windows. The use of grey ceramic tiles on the house, terrace, and pool basin aesthetically link these separate elements.

The pool has colored LED spotlights, and includes an underwater skimmer, a stainless steel ladder, and ceramic stairs.

This mansion sits in a 6000m² garden on the northern coast of Barcelona. The property's clear geometric lines (similar to the geometrical French / Provence or Italian-style gardens) are connected by travertine covered paths and stairs.

Garden plants were selected depending on their distance to the house, the type of the terrain, the view, and any other existing elements.

The 14m x 7m heated pool is bordered with artificial stone, beyond which an ipe-wood sundeck was constructed. The color of the water can be changed via twelve remote-control operated underwater LED spotlights. Using ultraviolet light and liquid oxygen are used to disinfect the pool, while the pH levels are adjusted automatically. Water cascades from three stainless steel "taps" with independent motors – these have timers. The pool also includes a counter current system.

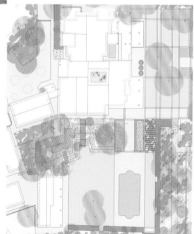

The 2.29m x 5.79m jacuzzi (model A.F.S. 19-DT) features a double heating system, a whirlpool air-water system, chromotherapy, and ozonization. Its ipe-wood cover matches the decking.

Situated on a steep hill over Costa Brava in northern Spain, this infinity-edge pool boasts spectacular views to the sea and surrounding bays. The sloped site was essential when creating the garden, as it was dominated by the rectangular 10m x 3m pool.

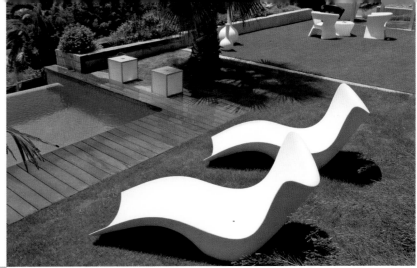

The heated pool is clad in small glass mosaic tiles. Colorful underwater illumination lends itself to chromotherapy; this uses the positive effects of light and color to sustain, relax, refresh, and recover the body. The pool is cleaned using salt electrolysis and underwater skimmers.

This utilitarian 20m x 2m infinity-edge pool built on a long, steep-graded 900m² lot had to be entirely integrated with the house in order to be structurally viable. The outward-facing side is slightly raised (more so than the interior-facing side), making it appear as if the pool is floating in mid-air.

The pool consists of one single lane that runs along the side of the lot, beside the house; the main focal point of this project is the water window at the far end of the structure. Red glass mosaic tiles enhance the aesthetic. The pool also includes underwater illumination and automatic cleaning nozzles.

The pool mirrors the house's irregular, asymmetrical structure, and the large window at the facade lines up directly with the water window.

The wooden terrace was built on a light metal structure, and includes a staircase that continues down to the pool.

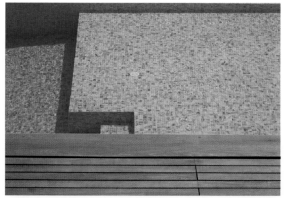

Below the main terrace, the 18.18m x 3.6m infinity-edge pool seems to melt into the horizon. A sundeck that protrudes from the pool has panoramic views of the bays of Costa Brava.

The basin, the walls, and the overflow canal of this rectangular pool are clad in glass tiles, while the lateral "relaxation area" is made of ipe wood. Four 300W underwater spotlights illuminate the pool. Other features include: a stainless steel ladder, an integrated automatic floor cleaner, a pump and sterilization unit, and solar heating.

This rectangular 60m² pool is clad in green / turquoise mosaic tiles, and features underwater illumination. A pond with water lilies sits directly below the infinity edge, but is not connected to the pool. Large granite tiles surround the terrace, while an ipe-wood platform serves as a sundeck.

Old pomegranate trees beside the natural pond serve to contrast the straight, minimalistic forms of the pool, house, and terrace.

The steep sloping terrain of this site meant that the designers had to place the pergola, pool, and deck on the highest level. All terraces offer unbeatable sunset views over the harbour.

This 11m x 3m infinity-edge pool was constructed using reinforced concrete, and is accessible via an elongated row of concrete stairs – the basin itself is painted white, while a turquoise feature wall toward the back can be seen from the harbour, and emphasizes the dark ipe-wood sundeck. The pool is illuminated by three spotlights, and cleaned using chlorine.

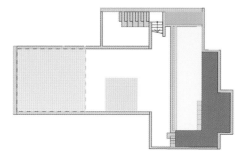

This rectangular 25m² stainless steel pool – with integrated stairs – punctuates a small wooden terrace with an ipe-wood sundeck. A garden bed and a stone wall visually protect the swimmers, while the stainless steel basin enhances underwater illumination. The pool cover is manual and easy to open and close.

This 32m² trapezoidal pool was designed to take advantage of spectacular views to Lake Luzern, and the Swiss Alps. The double infinity-edge is oriented to this direction, as are the stairs.

The pool is made of shotcrete and clad in stoneware tiles. Granite paving slabs envelop the terrace, while vertical granite plates at the garden's border are both decorative, and functional – they visually protect the space, but permit views to the landscape from the garden. The pool integrates underwater illumination and saline purification.

This 40m² pool belongs to a Minimalist house designed by architect Carlos Ferrater. The garden's openings and patios seek to communicate with the visual axis of the interior. The large outdoor area is divided into two U-shaped zones that embrace the house; the higher level (at the entrance) extends to the pool and to the sundeck. An expanse of lawn unifies these two separate areas, while the inclusion of native trees adds a sense of verticality to the overall aesthetic. The grey stoneware terrace tiles (45cm x 90cm) parallel the white ceramic tiles on the house's facade resulting in a space where garden, pool, and home form a harmonic unit.

The long rectangular pool – clad in white mosaic tiles – faces one of the interior patios and features full-side entrance stairs. Eight water jets build a decorative water cascade at one end. The pool also incorporates underwater illumination, and skimmers.

NATURA

POOLS

Pure crystalline water surrounded by plants, river stones, and other natural elements is an attractive concept in landscape composition, offering multiple possibilities for play and comfort.

Natural lakes and ponds are landscape elements that can not be transferred. The solution: to reproduce these natural elements on a scale suitable to residential properties, using natural cleansing to create recreational bathing areas and ornamental ponds.

Any water surface, regardless of its size, will accumulate particles from the surrounding area. This results in the development of microorganisms, which feed on these particles. Plants feed on what the microorganisms produce, and thus the links making up the chain of life begin. The attraction of this particular type of aquatic form is that it is a living system.

By using suitable substrates and plants, and by causing the water to move in a way that fosters ideal conditions, an equilibrium can be reached to keep the water crystalline and healthy. These conditions can be achieved without the use of traditional artificial treatments (chemical procedures such as chlorine and salt, or physical ones like UV radiation or ultrasound) meaning that the water can be considered "naturally purified" and suitable for a healthier and safer recreational bathing experience.

There are a multitude of reasons why people choose natural pools. Some are attracted to the chemical-free experience. Purified water is not only safer, but has beneficial effects on the skin, hair, and eyes. Others are interested in ecologically sensible alternatives to chlorinated pools.

People also have the option to select a specific level of maintenance: for plants that bloom at a certain time of year, or for more colorful contributions, or for plants native to their region.

The purification technique used will define the relationship between the purification area and the swimming area. The less technical the involvement, the greater the water surface-area dedicated to purification has to be to ensure a stable equilibrium that creates healthy, crystalline water. If little technology is applied, it is estimated that at least 120 square meters is needed with 60% of the surface area dedicated to purification. In this case, the investment is reduced because it is limited to sculpting the terrain, making it impermeable, and putting in a substrate and suitable

# NATURA

plants. During planning and construction, it must be ensured that the area is completely impermeable to prevent the continuous inclusion of water or earth from outside sources.

The technological input can be increased with the use of selected substrates and the forced controlled circulation of water. This will lead to a reduction of the swimming area, while the proportion dedicated to purification will drop to 5% of the total.

The water in the purification area needs to be replaced as it evaporates; adding or changing it for no reason means that the area will require a

period of time to acclimatize to the input of new elements.

The gravel or substrates used increase the water contact surface, which increases the space for purifying microorganisms, or biofilm, to develop. Plants purify by converting the particles in the water into green material, and by creating a favourable situation (in their roots) for the development of biofilm; this, in turn, helps by making nutrients available to the plants.

Water purified by natural means is a living system and therefore attractive to insects and animals that inhabit similar environments. If there are frogs in the vicinity, then frogs will come. Dragonflies are also common, and tend to be welcome as their larvae eliminate the presence of mosquitoes. Any technology that has been integrated into a purifying area will reduce the level of nutrients needed to create an equilibrium, meaning that insects and animals will not be able to find sustenance, and will leave.

Reproducing nature on a small scale has always been the objective of landscape architects; in this case biology and careful system engineering have been brought together to create something clean, functional, and safe.

L POOLS

This manicured and architecturally stylish garden has an outstanding element: the swimming pool, which extends from the bottom of the house like a delicate turquoise carpet. Large blocks of grey limestone (1.5m x 1m and 8cm thick) surround the pool, creating a sleek, contemporary aesthetic. Hosta flowers line the length of the pool, and lead to a boxwood terrace at the far end. Via the pool a visual axis has been created between the garden and the house.

The pool's design integrates the latest technology; it does not require the use of chemicals for its maintenance. This was achieved by incorporating a filtering system and a regeneration pond on one side of the garden, separate from the basin, leaving the architectural lines of the pool untouched.

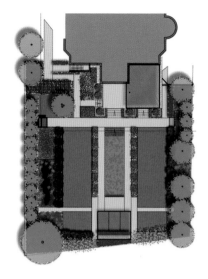

A filtering system with plants and sand work to remove phosphates, and result in transparent, completely clean water free of seaweed and other impurities. A pavilion at the end of the garden serves as a refuge in summer.

This naturalized pool by Daldrup is a pioneer project: the swimming area is separated from the filtering and purifying area. The filtration area includes a gravel garden, while the purifying pond (with fish) is surrounded by plants. These additions convey how aesthetically vibrant elements were incorporated into the design of functional areas.

Originally, this big country house – that dates back to 1730 – had stables and a barn. After years of use it was abandoned, and after World War II it was used as a warehouse for agricultural machines and farm appliances. It was not before the 80s that the current owner bought the estate and renewed the property, adapting it to modern times and residential use.

A path lined by linden and colorful hydrangeas leads to the pool. Boxwood spheres around the perimeter are complemented by countryside views and ruins recovered by antique dealers, while a wooden deck at the far end holds chairs, a table, and a picturesque summerhouse.

This large, irregular shaped pool is chemical free, and utilizes natural methods for cleaning and filtering, protecting swimmers' skin and eyes. A specialized pump system pushes the water through an area of gravel and aquatic plants, which filters and purifies. This system has been used in Germany, Austria, and Switzerland for more than fifteen years, with spectacular results.

The owner of this project requested that an authentic creek was integrated into the garden along with a modern pool, resulting in an outdoor space that consists of two distinct areas.

The 5m x 10m pool was constructed with a slight inclination (of 2m x 3m) for easier access; it features underwater illumination, an overflow canal, and is surrounded by granite slabs. Chip combustion heats the water.

The creek (50m long, and up to 4m wide) starts in a fountain basin above the pool where the water is pumped by inlet nozzles. It was designed to resemble a real Austrian creek: rocks and stones from the surrounding countryside and bed load material from the nearby quarries were brought to the site. Spotlights run the length of the creek, while three bridges (two granite, one wood) were built to facilitate accessibility.

The creek bed and the pool bottom were constructed with concrete. Above this a fleece layer and fabric-reinforced PVC foil serve as protection under the stone facade. Under the garden shed a large pump room services both the pool and the creek. Another room with three bronze pumps is tucked under the natural pool from which the creek flows and regulates (in three steps) the quantity of water and the current.

This elegant 2000m² garden has an expansive entrance and includes natural stone terraces and quartzite paths, a pavilion, a small gravel beach, and boxwood terraces. Its perimeter is studded with an eyecatching selection of white flowering plants, and maple and kazura.

The 32m² pool is framed by larch wood, while a wooden staircase leads into the completely transparent water. Three frogs live in the surrounding pond – a testament to the purity of the water – which is made accessible by the inclusion of wooden bridges.

Natural stone quartzite terraces provide spaces to relax and sunbath, and take in the garden's different decorative points: the lush, colorful greenery, the fountain, the stone table, and the banks distributed all over the garden. A pavilion was constructed in the far corner so that the owners could enjoy the garden and pool during winter. Paths are covered with large quartzite slabs, adding to the sense of space by making the garden's dimensions seem larger than they actually are.

This 60m² concrete pool in the countryside combines tradition with modern design. The lawn and woods around the house were refined with the inclusion of rhododendron at the garden borders and a rose garden. The pool has two infinity-edges (towards the 50m² purifying area), a platform made of exotic ipe wood, and a gangway of concrete slabs (1m x 40cm). It is lit using indirect and underwater illumination. The axis of the swim canal is aligned with the view from the living room, creating a direct connection between inside and out.

The lower section of this 1000m² garden integrates a natural pool that reflects the rectangular structures of the agricultural fields nearby, while the irregular shaped, overflow-style pool (with ipe-wood decking) sits 80cm higher than the upper level. This open area is exposed to the wind and weather; as a result a bathing area was created to provide shelter and protection. Old walls of natural stone remain at the garden borders.

The 25m² natural pool is a regeneration area with plants and gravel, and sits 0.8m lower than the surface – further protection is provided by gabion walls. A teak platform on one side provides a space to relax beside the water, while the stainless steel fountain at the edge contrasts and emphasizes the natural materials used.

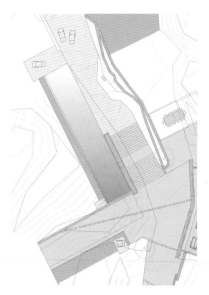

Surrounded by Mediterranean pine trees and taking advantage of a small piece of land, this swimming channel was set up using naturally-purified water. The owners' love of swimming, water, and nature led to the incorporation of a highly evolved biological purification strip; the filtered water streams out of a stone wall (mimicking a natural spring) at the far end of the pool. To emphasize the natural setting, an area was set up with ornamental water plants. This 40cm deep space has a layer of river gravel 0.4 to 4cm thick as well as two pumps that collect the leaves that fall into the water.

The site comprises two terraces. On the lower level, the 19m long rectangular swimming pool has a water surface of 75m². On the upper level, the 20m² purifying area includes a gravel bed and purifying plants fed by calibrated water circulation equipment. As the water travels through the purification area it retains all of its natural properties, and transparent color. The process includes no chemical treatments. This cleaning method is a reproduction of the biological processes of lakes and rivers, but on a smaller scale.

This project has been adapted to the landscape: it incorporates local stone and Mediterranean wood, allowing it to blend seamlessly with its surrounds.

Located in an old, unused basalt quarry in Madrid, this chemical-free natural pool (up to 14m below ground level) had to be designed and adapted to its surrounds. The construction was difficult due to the morphology and the characteristics of the ground: a gateway had to be built to reach the bio filter and plant area perched in the wall. Canals were installed so that rainwater could not enter the pool, and pumps were inserted into holes in rocks to conduct and recirculate water. A whirlpool sits up high, while two water features cascade into, and sit independent from, the pool – these different levels open up to spectacular views of the landscape.

This 28m² natural pool – with an irregular geometric shape – has been perfectly integrated into this elegant modern garden in Berlin. The 18m² purifying area – which incorporates water lilies and other aquatic plants – sits beside the bathing area, and is cleverly hidden from view by a natural stone wall.

A range of materials complements the sophisticated architectural design of the house. Underwater LED illumination adds character and a limestone platform protrudes like an island into the pool, while an ipe-wood deck provides an area to sunbathe. Corten steel borders on the lawn and pathways enhance the contemporary feel.

This large 40m² kidney-shaped pool is accessed via an ipe-wood platform. The 25m² purifying area encircles the bathing area, and is surrounded by a pebble beach and a scattering of boulders, which delineates it from the lawn.

The deck is partly covered by a stone pergola, which forms a shaded sitting area. A windowed garden house nestles into the terrace and serves as a storage area.

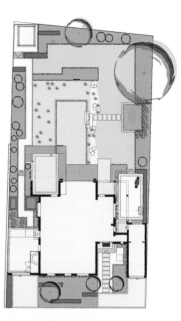

The complete renewal of this 1000m² garden was coordinated with the renovations made on the house. The owners wished to introduce modern forms and straight lines, but wanted a space that was also friendly and inviting.

This natural swimming pool includes a pea-gravel beach and a water fountain, as well as a sundeck visually protected by hedge segments. The water – which does not drop below 18°C – is regenerated without chemicals, and has an abundance of plant (reeds and lilies) and animal life. This area is dotted with diabese boulders, while stainless steel straps line the gravel paths.

Square granite slabs lead to a higher platform of Bangkirai wood surrounded by stones. Lavender behind the deep blue water fountain (positioned directly opposite the living room) brings color and elegance to the space

Situated on a hill, this garden has fantastic views to the valley below. The lake-like 60m² pool has an integrated purifying area (40m²) that incorporates gravel of different sizes, as well as water lilies, reeds, and other aquatic plants. The pool edge is lined with rocks and pebbles to separate it from the rest of the garden.

A stainless steel ladder on the ipe-wood deck complements the stainless steel shower, while a pier crosses the pool and continues to form a path to the house. A small maple tree, which turns red in autumn, is reflected in the pool, while the far end of the garden is scattered with large oak trees.

With a combination of quality materials and tremendous views, this sloped garden is a haven of relaxation. When this 3000m² garden was renewed, it was clear that the old pool and the pond had to be replaced. The result: an authentic deep green natural pool (20m²), complemented by abundant plant life, an ipe-wood sundeck, and a fitness area.

Large grey slate tiles surround the pool, while concrete stairs act as a functional minimalist counterpoint to the plantation. A stainless steel gargoyle adds character to this spectacular setting.

When re-forming the existing garden, a hub was created around the newly installed pool. This "living pool" looks like a conventional pool, but is in fact a fully-fledged biological pool. It does not utilize chlorine or other chemicals, nor does it incorporate flora and fauna.

A biological circulation system was incorporated, consisting of a biological filter (which uses bacteria to decompose organic impurities), a small pump, and a phosphorus filter (PhosTec Ultra). All components are integrated into a single shaft. This shaft (2.0m x 1.2m) is installed in the ground beside the existing pool and is connected to both its intake and outflow pipe. The bio circulation pump requires only a small amount of electricity.

Panoramic views over fields, lilac, a light cube at the far end of the pool and grey slate tiles on the terrace create an aesthetically pleasing space, while the Bangkirai wood sundeck (which will grey over time) is one of the owners' favourite places in the 2000m² garden.

This 80m² rectangular pool, constructed at the end of a sloped garden, has an irregularly shaped natural purifying area that sits directly beside the swimming basin. Within the 50m² purifying area a platform made of granite slabs juts out to create an island-like space, while a gravel beach delineates this area from the lawn.

The pool can be entered via a stainless steel ladder, or cement stairs, both of which stem from the wooden decks that surround the pool. The terrace is paved with 80cm² cement tiles.

This 900m² garden was designed on two levels: the L-shaped pool sits on the lower level, while the filter area (14m²) sits above it. Water cascades from the purification area into the main pool via coquina stone, while the Bangkirai wood sundeck is complemented by limestone slabs at intervals. Twenty spotlights illuminate the area. The purification area has a mechanism that allows it to switch from the "water cascade" function to an overflow-style function.

INDOOR

POOLS

An indoor pool is personal; it is an interior feature rather than an exterior feature and, as such, remains independent of climatic condition, and free from outdoor dirt and pollution.

Indoor pools are somewhat limited architecturally – they must adhere to the particular aesthetic dictated by the house in which they were built, while the materials and / or theme employed must be in accordance with the building. Thus indoor pools become artistic objects – that must work in unison with other elements – as well as functional objects.

The pool could be located in a separate or adjoining building. This way the building adapts to the pool and not the other way round. Indoor pools enclosed in glass or plastic structures are certainly more flexible in terms of aesthetic preferences. These structures

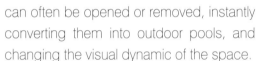

can often be opened or removed, instantly converting them into outdoor pools, and changing the visual dynamic of the space.

An indoor pool can be situated anywhere in a house: in the basement, in the attic, or adjacent to living spaces. Basement pools require the use of artificial light, although it is possible to make use of sunken gardens, which contribute natural light and help with ventilation. If the pool is installed on an upper level, floor-to-ceiling windows can be employed to showcase the view / landscape, and to make the space seem larger.

Fitness facilities often include indoor pools, especially in wellness areas. These are usually complemented by whirlpool spas and infrared lights, while floor heating adds a touch of luxury.

INDOOR

Indoor pools are a major cost, especially in regards to maintenance, water, and air temperature. They also require good ventilation systems. Indoor pools produce a great deal of humidity; if they are not isolated or properly contained, this can aversely affect other rooms in the building.

The dimensions and shapes are defined by the available space, especially for pools installed in basements. In some cases, an indoor pool functions as a swim canal, in others it has been designed for leisure and relaxation.

Flooring, whether ceramic or stone, needs to be anti-slip, while basins – like those of other pool types – tend to be clad in glass mosaic tiles.

The majority of these installations have little access to natural daylight, while some incorporate no daylight at all. Modern LED technologies offer a spectacular range of illumination styles. These have evolved to become elegant, sleek, and clean, quite different to the disco-light effect that was common during the early stages of LED technology. In general, the lighting that accompanies indoor pools is soft and indirect, although colored spotlights are growing in popularity.

POOLS

This private 4m x 20m heated pool is situated on the lower level of a large contemporary house styled by architect Carlos Ferrater. It features a counter current system and sidelong underwater illumination, and is cleaned using salt electrolysis. An interior patio – with four macro bonsais – provides the area with abundant daylight.

The pool basin is clad in white stoneware tiles, while the walls of the room are tiled with larger slabs. The ceiling is lined with ipe panels, and spotlights run along its entire length.

The swimming area is accompanied by a Finnish sauna as well as a 2m² jacuzzi with the same tiled effect as the pool. The wellness area is equipped with two massage chairs. A fully equipped fitness room opens to the pool.

This 12m x 2.5m heated pool was designed to be used as a swim canal. The shotcrete basin is clad in white glass mosaic tiles, which emphasize the underwater illumination; a small jacuzzi was designed in the same style. The purifying system disinfects the water using a chemical treatment.

The walls are finished in black slate edged with metal while the upper half is painted red. Built-in spotlights punctuate the black ceiling. This sleek and sophisticated interior is complemented by a daybed made of two chaiselongues, additional wind lights, dimmed lights, and small lighting strips in the floor, which give the hall a Japanese Zen touch.

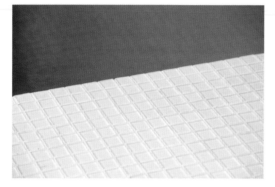

This 50m² heated pool emerges from the foundations of the house, and is accessible via the main garden and a small staircase. The teak decking that surrounds the pool and stretches to the lawn adds warmth and texture to the overall aesthetic.

A bespoke polyurethane cover protects the pool area. This enclosure is divided into three parts, and can be opened with sliding doors.

The irregular-shaped pool has a basin clad in blue glass mosaic tiles, an automatic floor cleaner, and underwater spotlights, as well as an eye-catching stainless steel water cascade.

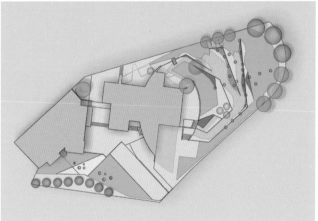

This interior pool is situated in a large country estate (owned by the same family for several generations) in Catalonia, between Barcelona and Girona. The Catalan farmhouse – once used for cattle breeding – was converted into a country house and, more recently, was transformed into a small wellness hotel.

The pool was built in the former stables on the ground floor of the house. Due to the age of the building and the rocky ground, security and permeability issues were important during the installation in order to avoid future problems. Traditional Catalan touches, like terracotta tiles, brick arches, and natural stone walls complete the overall aesthetic.

The 3.5m x 7.5m Moroccan-style pool has a painted shotcrete basin, and incorporates solar heating so it can be used on cold winter days when the outdoor pool is not available. The water is purified using salt chlorination, while halogen spotlights illuminate the underwater area. A sauna and relaxation area complement the pool, while a spiral staircase connects the wellness area with a main suite.

This 30m² rectangular pool was built on a sloped garden and creates a common space on the lower level, where the house opens up to the garden.

The garden was designed as an extension of the house; the intention was to bring nature and the seasons into semi-interior spaces. The pool is housed in a well-ventilated glass-pane structure supported by steel pillars and concrete slabs. The panes, which can be opened in summer, make it possible to convert the indoor pool into an outdoor pool.

This chlorinated pool was constructed using concrete covered with micro cement. It has underwater spotlights, a stainless steel ladder, and is heated.

Pale wood surrounds the perimeter of the pool, and enhances the vibrancy of the blue-green water; grey micro cement on the terrace emphasizes the black gravel used throughout the garden. A white greenhouse shade cloth protects the terrace in summer.

A mirror-effect ceiling made of stretched vinyl can be seen throughout Nick Spa & Sport Club in Barcelona, Spain.

The stainless steel jacuzzi includes a video projector which screens underwater photos and videos.

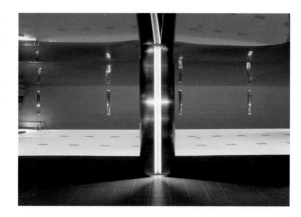

The large, 12m x 9m stainless steel spa was constructed using shotcrete, and has an irregular shape. The basin has lumbar jets and hot tubs, and offers hydro massage. Underwater illumination and a specialized thermally heated area are some of the spa's standout features.

The 20m x 6.5m indoor pool was also constructed of shotcrete and has an rectangular shape. The water is treated using low salt electrolysis, ultraviolent lamps, and glass filters. The pool is automatically cleaned and features underwater illumination.

When the garden was re-formed the owners installed a pool against the back wall of the house. This 8m x 3m rectangular pool is completely enclosed and, as such, can be used during colder months. The panels of the enclosure can be opened in summer. The stainless steel infinity-edge pool was made to measure, and also includes stainless steel stairs. The glass roof makes it possible to sky-watch while swimming.

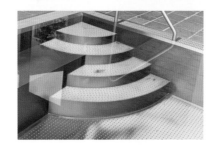

This project is located in a Modernist house. A brick water cascade situated at the end of the garden leads water, via a canal, to the pool, which sits 1m below the garden level. Two separate circuits have been integrated so this water does not mix with the pool water. This concept is a tribute to Arabic and Mediterranean gardens.

Garden and pool are situated on different levels. The circular shaped pool is 4.5m in diameter, and is accessed via a semi-circle of steps reminiscent of a theatre or Roman arena. These stairs, together with the grass that grows on them, create a singular space more oriented to conversation and relaxation than sports. This is perhaps why the owners equipped the pool with jacuzzi functions. The basin was made using shotcrete and is clad in blue glass mosaic, which complements the shiny Teca wood deck.

RUSTIC

POOLS

Rustic pools are frequently found in weekend homes, country homes, or in the mountains; almost always in idyllic locations related to leisure. The types of homes associated with rustic pools have often been in families for generations, but are no longer required for farming or agricultural purposes. They often undergo intensive reforms that see existing facilities repaired, redesigned, or removed. A water basin that is no longer used for its original purpose can be transformed into a family pool. A stable formerly used for cows and horses can be converted into a playing room, or into a living room. The

owners are almost always interested in the recovery or maintenance of the building's heritage, the environment, and in the preservation of a traditional aesthetic.

One of the most important decisions to make is the type of depuration system to integrate. Those who are environmentally conscious will favor a natural depuration system with plants and gravel (as described in the Natural Pools section). Another option is chemical or mechanical purification. Aquatic fauna is often present in rustic pools in rural environments. Small animals tend to drink from pools and algae may appear due to the contribution of nutrients from nearby fields. Whatever depuration system is chosen, it will need constant and efficient maintenance.

Most owners of rustic or classic pools opt for rectangular, traditional shapes, or irregular, organic shapes. The exterior perimeter of the pool may include natural stone walls that can be used as benches, or to sunbathe.

RUSTIC

Rustic pools are easily integrated into the garden landscape with the addition of fountains, man-made creeks, large plants, or boulders reminiscent of mountain rivers.

A variety of poolside accessories are utilized to complement rustic pools: garden pavilions with tables and chairs, wooden pergolas with Balinese beds, sundecks with rattan furniture, and shade-cloths made of natural fibre. Decorative objects like amphorae, old lanterns, terracotta flowerpots, sculptures, or art objects can also be incorporated to stylize the space.

Basins are usually clad in glass mosaic tiles of different colors (especially green and marine blue), and / or ceramic floor tiles. To add a rustic touch, images are sometimes embedded into the pool floor using tiles, or decorative edges are added. The border of the pool is usually constructed using natural or traditional stones from the region (granite, slate, etc.) contiguous to terraces, walls, or built-in furniture of the same material. Rustic pools do not often include underwater spotlights, but if they do, they are usually white in color, and tie-in with the general illumination in the garden.

The prevailing colors in these installations are strong earthly shades like yellow, ochre, rust, and brown, all of which contrast and emphasize the emerald green or marine blue water and tiles.

POOLS

This garden, on an idyllic country estate close to the French border, features two pools. A natural pond – watered by an old creek that passes through the grounds – flows into a traditional water basin. The landscapers integrated a wooden platform to create a relaxing shaded space, although the pond itself is not used for swimming.

In an old meadow an outdoor pool (with a water surface of 70m²) was constructed with integrated brickwork stairs and small blue glass mosaic tiles which complement the underwater illumination feature. The surrounding sundeck of traditional Catalan terracotta tiles (30cm²) will develop a patina in time.

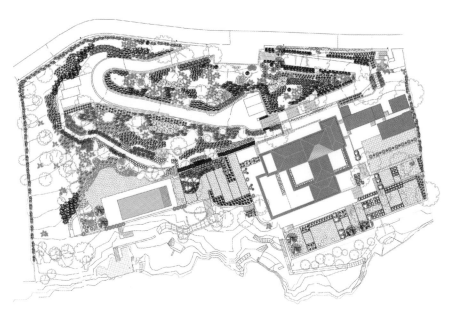

This picturesque, romantic garden overlooking Mallorca's Formentor bay opens to 360-degree views of the sea. The sloping terrain is edged with natural stone walls that were locally sourced, and constructed by Mallorcan artisans using traditional methods. The 50m² infinity-edge pool is bordered by Italian terracotta pots and incorporates evocative green marble tiling and underwater illumination. It also includes an automatic floor-cleaning system.

This rectangular pool (6m x 12m) belongs to an old restored country house, and was built in place of the original stables, of which two walls have been conserved. The pool has a salt depuration system and an automatic skimmer, and features underwater illumination, as well as emerald green glass mosaic tiles. Cane deckchairs, and a long stone bench (with bespoke white leather cushions) complement the sandstone terraces and pine trees that surround the area.

The garden is separated from an adjacent golf course by a 10cm wall; this delineates the property line while retaining the continuity of the landscape, and facilitates breathtaking views of the Pyrenees and the Empordà plains. A series of cut-away terraces create different levels (much like the agricultural fields of the area): the first is a lawn area directly beside the pool; the second is a rustic, prairie-like level that includes climate-resistant plants.

The pool design corresponds to that of an old farmhouse water tank. It has a trapezoidal shape and slate walls, while the ceramic basin is light green in color, and visually fuses the pool with the landscape. Design elements include a wooden sundeck which looks like a pier.

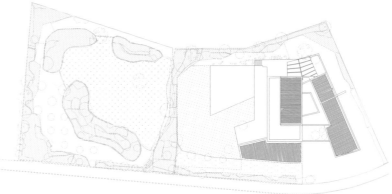

This 6000m² contemporary garden – that surrounds a chalet on the northern coast of Barcelona – plays with colors, shapes, and sculptures.

The infinity-edge pool (16m x 8.5m) was built on the highest level of the terrain, and was constructed using shotcrete and green glass tiles. The water is cleaned using salt electrolysis.

A decorative, mushroom-shaped spring can be seen from the living room of the house; its functions (water level and flow power) can be programmed and regulated. The water travels to the pool via a glass fibre canal clad in black tiles. At the opposite end a sculpture by Sabine Morvan fuses with the pool and the ocean in the background. The pool sits between two metal pavilions that offer shade and panoramic views, and features an ipe-wood sundeck with 10cm-wide panels.

The estate – which includes a Modernist residential villa dating from 1906, and a park area with a servant's house – is situated in an exclusive residential area in Munich. The garden has a pavilion with a chimney and a dining area; depending on the time of year, it serves as either a summerhouse, or a conservatory.

The pool (10m x 4m) was positioned at the southern side of the facade and sits flush with the surrounding pathway and the lawn. It includes a counter current system and is clad in green Andeer granite slabs from Switzerland. Particularly striking are four springs in the form of lion heads carved out of Italian sandstone.

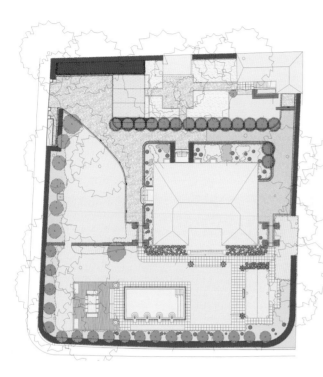

Opposite the pavilion, a sundeck of red cedar wood is situated on a slightly higher level. Classical-style columns support the porch and are complemented by limestone pavers from Nuremberg. The garden has a sunnier area as well as a shaded area defined by ivy plants, small pathways, and sculptures. At night the pool, garden, and summerhouse / conservatory are illuminated.

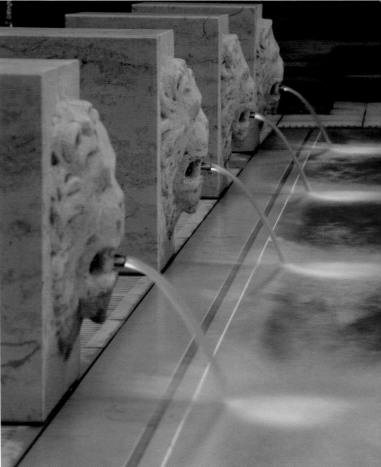

This haven of peace in the Spanish countryside is an elegant combination of past and present. The 80m² rectangular pool – with a round entrance staircase – is one of the main attractions in this country garden, and is the principal nexus between inside and outside. The lawn is completely clear of plants so as not to obstruct the views from the pool to the house, and vice versa, while the flowering plants around the perimeter of the garden are blue, matching the pool's glass mosaic tiles.

A dolphin mosaic on the pool basin and decorative edging that reflects off the water complement the terracotta tiled border and the stone used to construct the house. Water streams into the pool from the mouths of small ceramic frogs situated along the border. Three stone flowerpots on the terrace enhance the rustic atmosphere.

This 18m x 5m rectangular pool accompanies a spectacular mansion on a 14,500m² estate on Mallorca Island. Although it sits beside a newly constructed garden house, its design incorporates natural stones (used in field walls across the island), old wooden beams, and emerald green mosaic tiles: a tribute to the traditional materials, and methods of construction that can be seen throughout the estate. The entrance and terrace floors were sourced from an old chapel on the island.

A stone wall separates the garden house from the pool – which also features underwater spotlights, and salt depuration – while a broad staircase leads into the water, and is reminiscent of old Roman bathhouses.

This 120-year-old mansion – situated in an isolated mountain area behind the coastline of the Costa Blanca, close to Altea – was built to resemble a castle. The grounds are surrounded by 43 hectares of almond and pine terraces.

The original house and garden were in a ruinous state, and had to be completely renovated. Inner and outer walls were constructed of natural stone; old oak beams were brought from France for the roof; while terracotta, produced in the nearby town of Denia, was used as paving. Amphorae, cast-iron furniture, and decorative antiques from nearby markets help conserve the rustic aesthetic.

The swimming pool (40m$^2$) was built by a local company, and was designed to mirror the rustic style of the house. It features a shotcrete basin clad in green mosaic glass tiles, and underwater spotlights, and integrates traditional salt cleaning. The far end incorporates an overflowing system.

When re-forming this garden, near the Roman ruins of Tarragona, a unique design element was integrated: three big amphorae now sit within arched recesses at one end of the pool.

The rectangular pool (10.6m x 3.6m) includes a variety of features, including: a shotcrete basin clad in glass mosaic tiles, an anti-slip finish on the steps and natural-stone edging tiles, an automatic filtering system (which has the ability to clean and recirculate the full water volume in four hours), purifying accessories (including nozzles and drains), an automatic disinfection element that pumps hypochlorite into the water as needed, and an automatic floor cleaning system – that includes eight nozzles in the floor, five nozzles in the stairs, and a 1.5in valve – that works in unison with the filtration equipment. It also incorporates a built-in skimmer system (along the whole width of the pool) that produces an overflowing effect. Underwater illumination comes via five projectors with stainless steel rings.

Pathways wind in and out of this lush, native-only garden, and terraces open to the spectacular panorama.

An infinity edge was integrated at one end of this 50m² irregular-shaped pool, while water cascades from a natural stone wall at the other. Big boulders were distributed around this area so that it resembles a natural lake. White and blue glass mosaic tiles complement the pool's functional features, which include: underwater illumination, a diving board, lateral entrance stairs, and an automatic floor cleaning system.

This 4m x 10m rectangular pool sits within a classical-style garden. It is symmetrically placed and faces the house. The area surrounding the perimeter of the pool and the terrace are tiled with dark granite slabs. Five large flowerpots delineate the pool from the garden.

The pool, which has a basin clad in white tiles, can be accessed via a lateral staircase and includes underwater spotlights. The pool cover is remote control operated, and works in unison with skimmers to keep the water clean.

This 500-year-old building was constructed over an old Jewish synagogue in the center of Pals, a medieval village in northern Spain. The house was restored and retains its natural stone walls and wooden beams, but incorporates technical advances such as running water, electricity, and heating. Concrete walls were painted with lime, while doors and openings were designed as arches.

The 3m x 8m swimming pool was constructed in the basement, is open to the sky, and is enveloped by wooden decking. The basin is clad in Italian Bisazza glass mosaic tiles.

Four small cypresses behind the pool and a patio decorated with colorful flowerpots, rugs, and candles evoke an Arabesque atmosphere.

This country home was built in the 17th century and restored in 2005 with an aim to maintain its rustic structure. The irregular shaped pool amalgamates three circles and is an exterior highlight that contrasts the old-world glamor of the house. Each circle has a different depth and diameter. The smallest imitates a beach.

The pool, which is clad in light blue glass mosaic tiles, is surrounded by stoneware slabs which merge with a wooden sundeck. It includes a counter current system and a water cascade that falls from a large rock at the border of the pool. From the pool, swimmers can enjoy panoramic views of the village and an old church nearby.

This irregular, egg-shaped pool – clad in light blue glass mosaic tiles – sits within the large terraced garden of a classic-style mansion. Terraces and pathways of Banyoles stone are complemented by terracotta pots and flowering plants closer to the house, while the perimeter of the garden is bordered with native pine trees and shrubs.

The special feature of this pool is a wooden island in its centre made accessible by the inclusion of a wooden bridge. From here swimmers can dive into the water or relax in the sun. The pool can be accessed via side ladders, a stainless steel springboard, or two slides, which form part of the children's playground.

This 3m x 7m rectangular pool belongs to a spectacular country house that was originally a barn. The architect maintained the structure's wooden beams, natural stone walls, arches, and pillars, as well as the terracotta flooring.

The pool sits on a lower level than the garden – where the animal stables used to be – and is separated from it by stairs and a natural stone wall. The pool includes underwater spotlights, a skimmer, and entrance stairs. The basin is clad in marine blue glass mosaic tiles. A large terracotta terrace for sunbathing is complemented by terracotta flower pots and rattan outdoor furniture, which enhances the rustic atmosphere.

This 8m x 3m rectangular pool – situated in the middle of the lawn – is surrounded by a platform made of tropical wood that helps connect different spaces within the garden. The same material was used for the decking that links the house with the pergola.

The pool is clad in emerald green glass mosaic tiles, and features underwater spotlights, side-stair entry, and an auto-cleaning skimmer as well as a salt depuration system. An outdoor shower is situated nearby.

This house evokes a country atmosphere, while the decorative features add a modern touch; cushions made of sackcloth, plastic sofas by Kartell, modern deckchairs, and an assortment of objects add subtle rustic touches to the space.

This 4m x 10m rectangular pool is situated in a rural area amongst almond and orange groves, and vineyards. The basin is clad in light blue glass mosaic tiles, which are emphasized by underwater spotlights. At the far end of the pool, a limestone solarium – situated beside a terrace with outdoor sofas – complements the limestone slab terrace around the perimeter of the pool.

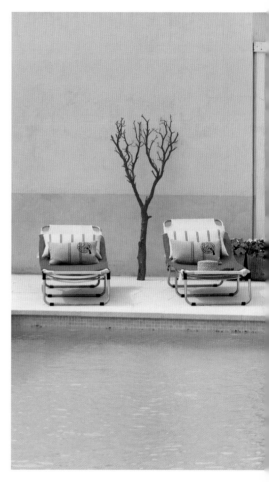

# Credits

## Modern Pools

### Page 10

**Location:** Sitges, Spain

**Designer:**
Architect: Paco Alonso Caballero
Torrent de l'olla, 82, Barcelona,
Spain
t +34 932102274
e alonsoarquitectes@
alonsoarquitectes.com
w www.alonsoarquitectes.com

**Pool builder:**
Exterior piscines
Ctra. St. Pere de Ribes 18-24,
08870 Sitges, Spain
t +34 938941466
w www.exteriorpiscines.com

### Page 12

**Location:** Santa Cristina de Aro,
Girona, Spain

**Designer:**
Architect: Xavier Canosa Magret
c/ Emili Grahit, Nº 62 E-1
E-17.003 Girona, Spain

**Pool builder:**
ATIPIC Girona S.L.
c/ de la Pau 6
E-17240 Llagostera, Girona, Spain
f +34 972805708
e info@atipicgirona.com
w www.atipicgirona.com

### Page 14

**Location:** close to Linz, Austria

**Designer and pool builder:**
Freiraum Gartenarchitektur GmbH,
"Gärtner von Eden"
Emling 29
A-4072 Alkoven
t +43 (0) 7274613440
e office@freiraum.cc
w www.freiraum.cc

### Page 18

**Location:** Lloret de Mar, Costa
Brava, Spain

**Pool design and builder:**
XYZ Piscinas
c/ Ganduxer 26, 2º-3ª
E-08021 Barcelona, Spain
t +34 932007547
e info@xyzpiscinas.com
w www.xyzpiscinas.com

### Page 20

**Location:** Sant Just, Barcelona,
Spain

**Pool builder:**
Jardineria Domenech – Jaume
Domenech
Avinguda de Josep Tarradellas
E-08225 Terrassa, Spain
t +34 605866276
e info@jardineria-domenech.com
w jardineriadomenech.com

**Landscape architect and pool
designer:**
Paula Rodrigues
t +34 625112988
e paula.exteriores@gmail.com

**Furniture:**
Sofas by Manutti

### Page 24

**Location:** north of Barcelona,
Spain

**Designer:**
Despatx d'arquitectura
Eduard Broto Comerma
c/ Sant Leopold, 27
E-08221 Terrassa, Spain
t +34 937889689
f +34 937337994

**Pool builder:**
XYZ Piscinas, S.L.
c/ Ganduxer, 26, 2º-3ª
E-08021 Barcelona, Spain
t +34 932007547
f +34 932006950
e info@xyzpiscinas.com
w www.xyzpiscinas.com

### Page 26

**Location:** Tossa de Mar, Costa
Brava, Spain

**Designer:**
Team: Jardí Mediterrani
Design by Xavier Danés: Adam
Martí, Xavier Danés, Jordi Mateu

**Pool builder:**
Xavier Danés
Jardí Mediterrani Girona-Lloret
Ronda Ferran Puig Nº 27
E-17001 Girona, Spain
t +34 972019130
e jardi@jardimediterrani.com

**Solar protection specialist:**
Jordi Mateu
Elements de protecció solar i
tancaments
Carretera Blanes Nº 147
E-Lloret de Mar, Spain
t +34 972363861

**Gandía Blasco-Kartell
showroom:**
Montserrat Royo
c/ Ramon Turró Nº 6
E-17005 Girona, Spain
t +34 972019128
e kartell@italyinteriors.com
w www.kartell.it

**Italy Interiors:**
Adam Martí
c/ Bernat Boades Nº 4
E-17005 Girona, Spain
t +34 972410503
e italy@italyinteriors.com
w www.italyinteriors.com

**Terrace furniture:**
Jardí Mediterrani.
Ronda Ferran Puig Nº 27
E-17001 Girona
t +34 972019130
e jardi@jardimediterrani.com

**Extra credits:**
Shower diffuser and foot washing
system by Hansgrohe:
www.hansgrohe.es
Illumination by Iguzzini:
www.iguzzini.com
Loudspeakers by Harman Kardon:
www.harmankardon.com
Domotic sun protection by Somfy:
www.somfy.es
Deck chairs and sofas
(Model: Na Xemena) by Gandía
Blasco: www.gandiablasco.com
Flower pots with integrated
illumination by Vondom:
www.vondom.com
Table (Model: 1-2) manufactured
by Zeritalia and designed by
Jean Nouvel
White leather sofas
(Model: James) by Casadessús
Lamp (Model: Bridge) by DARK

## Page 30
**Location:** Sant Cugat, Barcelona,
Spain
**Designer and pool builder:**
David Paricio
El Mon de la Piscina
Crta.N-II Km. 649
Maresme, Barcelona, Spain
t +34 937901588
e info@elmondelapiscina.com
w www.elmondelapiscina.com

**Extra credits:**
Natural stones by Bruc Jardí
Starfish and shells: handmade
claywork design by Maria Eugènia
Orenga

## Page 34
**Location:** Barcelona, Spain
**Designer:**
Architect: JEEV arquitectura
Carrer Xerric 21
E-08172 Barcelona, Spain
t +34 935441822
e estudi@jeev-arq.com
w www.jeev-arq.com

**Pool builder:**
Piscines del Vallés
c/ Bejar 46
08225 Terrassa
t +34 937359192
w www.piscinesvalles.com

**Extra credits:**
Floor tiles by Rosa Gres:
www.rosagres.com

## Page 36
**Location:** north of Barcelona,
Spain
**Designer and pool builder:**
Pool, jacuzzi, and waterfalls
"EL MON DE LA PISCINA"
David Paricio
Crta.N-II Km. 649
08301 Mataró, Barcelona, Spain
t +34 937901588
e info@elmondelapiscina.com
w www.elmondelapiscina.com

## Page 40
**Location:** Costa Brava, Spain
**Pool builder:**
Jardí Mediterrani Girona-Lloret
Xavier Danés
Ronda Ferran Puig Nº 27
E-17001 Girona, Spain
t +34 972019130
e jardi@jardimediterrani.com

**Solar protection specialist:**
Jordi Mateu
Elements de protecció solar i
tancaments
Carretera Blanes Nº 147
E-Lloret de Mar, Spain
t +34 972363861

**Gandía Blasco-Kartell
showroom:**
Montserrat Royo
c/ Ramon Turró Nº 6
E-17005 Girona, Spain
t +34 972019128
e kartell@italyinteriors.com
w www.kartell.it

**Italy Interiors:**
Adam Martí
c/ Bernat Boades Nº 4
E-17005 Girona, Spain
t +34 972410503
e italy@italyinteriors.com

**Extra credits:**
Daybed, lamps sofa, and table
(Model: Saler) by Gandía Blasco:
www.gandiablasco.com
Vase (Model: La Bohemme) by
Kartell: www.kartell.it
Chairs and table (Model: Pal) and
deckchairs (Model: Surf Lounger)
by Karim Rashid for Vondom
Flowerpots with integrated lights
(Collection: Moma) by Javier
Mariscal for Vondom
Flower pots by J.M. Ferrrero for
Vondom
Carpet (Collection: Cactus) and
cushions by Missoni

## Page 44

**Location:** Aiguaxelida, Costa Brava, Spain

**Designer and pool builder:**
ARCHIKUBIK
Architects: Marc Chalamanch, Miquel Lacasta, and Carmen Santana
c/ Luís Antunez Nº 6
E-08006 Barcelona, Spain
t +34 934152762
e info@archikubik.com
w www.archikubik.com

## Page 46

**Location:** Costa Brava, Spain

**Designer and Pool builder:**
Construccions Soler K-litat, S.L.
c/ Francesc Cambó 33
E-17310 Lloret de Mar, Spain
t +34 972349310
f +34 972108801
e info@solerklitat.com
w www.solerklitat.com

**Extra credits:**
Glass tiles: Libra Vitráico
Water heater: Torson F3 Wolf

## Page 50

**Location:** Madrid, Spain

**Designer:**
Luis Vallejo
LVEP Luis Vallejo Estudio de Paisajismo
Paseo de los Serbales 4, Urb Ciudalcampo
San Sebastian de los Reyes
28707 Madrid, Spain
t +34 916570954
e paisajismo@luisvallejo.com
w www.luisvallejo.com

**Pool builder:**
Arceval Jardineria
Paseo de los Serbales 4
E-28707 Ciudadelcampo, Spain
t +34 916570954

## Page 52

**Location:** Port Soller, Mallorca Island, Spain

**Designer and pool builder:**
Anke Scheideler and Roland Weber
DUO Soller S.L.
Gran Vía 22
E-07100 Soller, Mallorca Island, Spain
t +34 971634774
e mail@duo-concept.de
w www.duo-concept.de

**Extra credits:**
Exterior furniture: Duo Soller

## Page 56

**Location:** Linz, Austria

**Designer and pool builder:**
Freiraum Gartenarchitektur GmbH "Gärten von Eden"
Emling 29,
A-4072 Alkoven, Austria
t +43 (0) 7274613440
e office@freiraum.cc
w www.freiraum.cc

## Page 60

**Location:** Luzern, Switzerland

**Designer and pool builder:**
Müller Gartenbau AG "Gärtner von Eden" ®
Bruno Müller Götzentalstrasse 1
CH-6044 Udligenswil, Switzerland
t +41 (0) 413758050
e mail@mueller-gartenbau.ch
w www.mueller-gartenbau.ch

## Page 64

**Location:** Sant Cugat del Valles, Barcelona, Spain

**Designer:**
Architect: Carlos Ferrater
ARQUITECTOS ASOCIADOS
Balmes, 145 bajos
E-08008 Barcelona, Spain
t +34 932385136
e carlos@ferrater.com

**Pool builder:**
Construcciones Perez Villora,
Sant Joan Despí, Barcelona
w www.cpvsa.com

## Natural Pools

Text and advice on natural pools:
Ignacio Pujol, Ara Grup / Balena Group
t +34 937509450
e info@aragrup.es
w www.aragrup.es

## Page 72

**Location:** Bochum, Germany

**Designer:**
Kulmann-Rohkemper "Gärtner von Eden"
Langehegge 326,
D-45770 Marl, Germany
t +49 236542216
e info@kulmann.com
w www.kulmann.com

**Pool builder:**
Michael Daldrup "Gärtner von Eden"
Burg Hülshoff, Schonebeck 6
D-48329 Havixbeck, Germany
t +49 253464670
e info@daldrup.de
w www.daldrup.de

**Page 180**

**Location:** Altea, Costa Blanca, Spain

**Pool builder:**
Gunitados Eltx
**w** www.gunitadoselx.com

**Page 184**

**Location:** Tarragona, Spain

**Designer and pool builder:**
Grup Staff
Polígon Industrial Can Torrella
Ronda Shimizu, 8
E-08233 Vacarisses, Spain
**t** +34 938281830
**e** staff@staff.es
**w** www.staff.es

Page 188

**Location:** Pollensa, Mallorca Island, Spain

**Designer:**
Private owner of the estate

**Pool builder:**
Construction by local professionals

**Page 192**

**Location:** close to Lake Constance, Switzerland

**Designer:**
Erni Gartenbau + Planung AG
Christian Erni
Am Hafen
CH-8598 Bottighofen, Switzerland
**t** 0716771166
**e** info@erni-gartenbau.ch
**w** www.erni-gartenbau.ch

**Page 196**

**Location:** Pals, Empordà region, Spain

**Designer:**
Unknown

**Page 198**

**Location:** Empordà region, Gerona, Spain

**Designer:**
Owner and architect

**Page 202**

**Location:** Palamos, Gerona, Spain

**Designer:**
Marià Pradell
Jardineria Pradell S.L.
Buenos Aires, 6
E-08340 Vilassar, Barcelona, Spain
**t** +34 937593436
**e** jardpradell@terra.es

**Page 206**

**Location:** Empordà region, Gerona, Spain

**Designer:**
Daniel Lizarrituri

**Page 210**

**Location:** Sant Cugat, Barcelona, Spain

**Designer:**
Cristobal Catalan
GREEN LINE GARDENS
Avda. Juan XXIII Nº 12
E-08918 Badalona, Barcelona, Spain
**t** +34 933925657
**w** www.green-line.es

**Page 214**

**Location:** Pollensa, Mallorca Island, Spain

**Designer:**
Jaume Mestre
Mestre Paco S.L.
Can Berenguer
E-07460 Pollença, Balears, Spain
**t** +34 971534370
**e** mestrepaco@telefonica.net
**w** www.mestrepaco.com

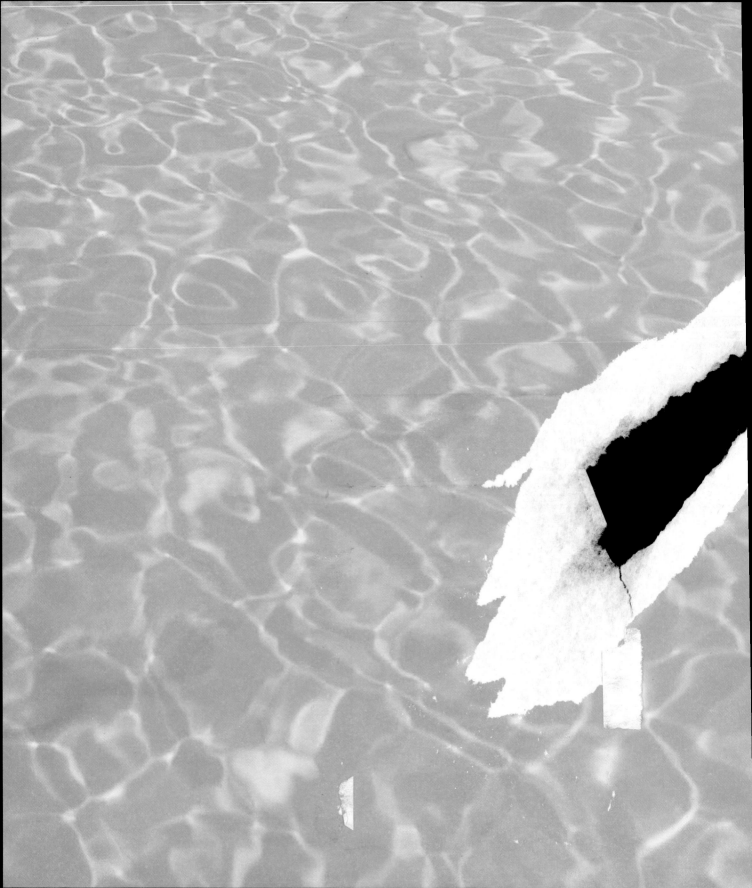